MERCEDES-BENZ
C 111

PAUL FRÈRE

MERCEDES-BENZ
C 111

EXPERIMENTAL CARS

Photographs by Julius Weitmann

EDITA LAUSANNE

This book was created and produced by Edita S.A. Lausanne

ISBN 2-88001-095-0

Printed and bound in Switzerland

CONTENTS

FOREWORD

This book bears the mark of a great photographer: Julius Weitmann. Unfortunately, although the Mercedes-Benz C 111 fascinated him above all other cars, he will never see this volume dedicated to it, for he died suddenly on September 21 1980, aged 72.

But I could very well visualise his reaction if he had this book, his creation, in his hands. He would not have shown the least self-congratulation, however justified; he would have simply turned the pages without a word, then, laconically, he might have uttered: 'You know, one could have perhaps made more of this picture.'

Compromise never existed in Julius Weitmann's vocabulary. His continual defence of his convictions did not make life easy for the people he worked with, nor for himself. Whether trying to capture the lines of a new model, or trying to freeze a moment of drama on a race track, Julius Weitmann had his own ideas and he fought for them.

I first met Julius Weitmann in 1954 when he turned up at the circuits with his Speed Graphic. My colleagues and I, who used compact cameras, never took him seriously, convinced that he could not possibly get action shots with a camera of that size. We couldn't have been more mistaken. Julius took some impressive race pictures, he saw men and their machines from new angles. He had the quality of a good reporter — being at the right place at the right time.

With extraordinary coolness he knew precisely when to release his shutter, to capture unforgettable pictures of the most thrilling moments; such as Richard von Frankenberg's Porsche in mid-air above the Avus corner, or Hans Herrmann flung out of his BRM on the same circuit.

Julius Weitmann leaves us thousands of sensational pictures — of cars, races and drivers — pictures which will remain a testimony to motor sport history.

This book on the C 111 was something out of the ordinary for him. Each of the pictures published here — chosen from among hundreds — is the result of craftsmanship in the real sense of the term. Julius understood better than anyone how to portray the challenge of the C 111, a machine described by Professor Werner Breitschwerdt, chief of research and development at Daimler-Benz, as an 'exploratory vehicle'.

In his heated discussions on every subject, Julius Weitmann was neither flexible nor obliging. But he hid a sensitive character under his harsh exterior, and at heart was a romantic, attached to the values of the past. I don't think anything could have given him more pleasure than the publication of this book, so typical of his style and which will perpetuate his memory.

Günther Molter

MERCEDES-BENZ C 111 EXPERIMENTAL CARS

It was at the press launch for a new Mercedes model in the late sixties. After dinner, a small group of motoring journalists sat at the table of Rudolf Uhlenhaut, who was then director in charge of car development at Daimler-Benz. We talked cars, of course, and very soon the inevitable question cropped up: "Why does Mercedes-Benz no longer engage in Formula One racing?" "Because we don't need it, and because we don't have time for it", replied Uhlenhaut, and then, with utter frankness, he added: "Also, racing car technique has changed so drastically during the past years that we no longer know whether we would be able to do better than the others".

A company of Daimler-Benz's repute, however, cannot afford to leave important aspects of automotive technology unexplored. In those days, development work on the Wankel rotary engine was intense, and this afforded a good opportunity to design and build a centrally-engined car, to try out the latest developments in suspension and plastics, as well as certain new ideas conceived by the company. This was a strong argument to justify the design of the C 111. Besides, development engineers deserve and need occasional distraction from their tedious routine work. A special project of this kind could have a stimulating effect as a sort of mental training.

Officially, the C 111 was nothing but a laboratory on wheels and it successfully fulfilled this function for many years. Many ideas tried out on this experimental car later found their way into series production.

It had been stipulated that the C 111 must not become a racing car in which, everything — comfort, silence, ease of access, and durability — takes second place to high performance. If the C 111 was to become an indicator of future design trends, the temptation to build it as a racing car would have to be resisted. Thus, it was designed as a genuine Grand Tourer, and just as much attention was paid to comfort and quiet running as to performance and road holding.

Furthermore, the construction had to be suitable, at least in principle, for limited series production. A company that prospered by producing several hundred cars a day should not, it was felt, build a one-off special, even as an experimental vehicle, without giving consideration to regular production techniques.

Another objective was research in the field of plastics for car body design, and testing the limitations of their use. Such a vehicle would have to have the best possible aerodynamic properties within the limits set by its Grand Touring concept. It was important not only to reduce the drag coefficient (C_R) as much as possible, but also to shape the body to avoid aerodynamic lift and to achieve — if possible — some aerodynamic downforce, because lift is detrimental to handling and safety at high speeds.

Once the Board of Directors had approved the C 111 project, Dr. Hans Liebold was put in charge of its development. Shortly afterwards he was appointed C 111 project manager. In the first months of 1969, the construction drawings were produced and the development department at Untertürkheim built the first body platform and the main chassis and suspension components.

It was not always easy to come to the right decision when choosing between the various possible technical solutions. The temptation to make the C 111 a thoroughbred sports racing car was great. It would have been easy to achieve the ultimate in lightness and performance to the detriment of suitability for normal road use, of series production feasibility and of durability. Doing that, however, would have meant missing part of the project's objective. It would have been possible to build a tubular frame on the lines of the erstwhile 300 SL. Yet this construction would have wasted both time and space; just think of the high door sills of the gull-wing SL. Similarly, an aluminium monocoque as used on most present formula and sports racing cars, would not have brought any experience useful to series production. Again, it must be emphasized that the real essence of the C 111 project was to gain experience relative to the products Mercedes were selling. Therefore, it was decided to opt for a welded steel platform with integrated steel bulkheads front and rear. The windscreen and rear window frames, connected by a longitudinal spar acted as a roll cage. The spar also supported the gull-wing doors. For the first time, computer aided design was applied to the support elements. Calculations were carried out in cooperation with IBM on the basis of the elasto-static element method. A tubular frame was designed from which the characteristics of a sheet steel platform frame of identical rigidity could be mathematically deduced.

In the hollows of the frame's side members, which also acted as door sills, two plastic-coated aluminium fuel tanks of 13 gallons each were installed to save space. This position offered the added advantage of keeping the car's centre of gravity low, and of minimising changes in axle loads while the tanks were being emptied.

In those days — 1969 — Daimler-Benz was about to discard the swing axle — a construction feature they had adhered to and improved upon for 35 years. Now, a semi-trailing arm rear suspension was adopted for the 'small' Series 107 Mercedes. It was intended to test this design to its limits by applying it to the C 111. As the car was to be alternatively equipped with radial, road tyres and wide, racing tyres, there were serious doubts as to whether the relatively large changes of track and wheel camber of this axle would be compatible with the wide and flat tyre contact area of modern racing tyres. On the other hand, this axle offered the advantage of an anti-dive effect.

The transverse links of the front suspension were also designed to counteract progressively the dive effect during braking. Thus, major castor changes and their negative effect on the steering as the springs compressed and extended, could be avoided. This was achieved by setting the axes of rotation of upper and lower transverse links at an angle to each other. Such an axle was used on the Series 107 with a rubber mounted subframe, thereby insulating the passenger compartment from road noise. It was intended to leave out the subframe to save weight and to attain greater steering precision without sacrificing sound insulation. A suspension system was finally designed which was essentially similar in its geometry to that of the Series 107. However, the transverse links were directly attached to the body platform, and the distance between the upper and lower transverse links was considerably increased. The result was a significant reduction of the forces — particularly braking forces — acting on the suspension, and this allowed the use of softer rubber bushes for the link attachment points. Consequently, the sound insulation was at least as good as on the subframe arrangement. Furthermore, steering precision was enhanced because of fewer rubber elements between the wheels and the body.

Three years later, this front suspension was adopted — virtually unchanged — for the S-Class Series 116 saloons. With some small improvements it still used on all Mercedes models today.

Although all racing and sports racing cars, including the exotic sports cars, featured rack and pinion steering, Daimler-Benz shunned this fashion and continued to use its own recirculating ball steering. It was not because of the lack of good rack-and-pinion steering suppliers that Mercedes came to this decision. Rather, it was felt that rack-and-pinion steering on a road car using extra wide tyres would transmit more road shocks to the steering wheel than was acceptable by Daimler-Benz.

Despite all the many technical innovations in various spheres, the main point of interest in the C 111 was the centrally-mounted three-rotor Wankel engine. In those days, Daimler-Benz technicians had great hopes for the future of the rotary engine. The Wankel unit featured prominently in the product plans for the mid-seventies, and its development was vigorously encouraged. This was before the stringent exhaust emission regulations which hampered Wankel development. And then came the oil crisis which put paid to any further development of rotary engines.

The three-rotor engine was based on the original NSU design, from whom a patent licence had been obtained. Each rotor had a chamber volume of 600 cc and there was an alloy block with cast steel rotors and cast iron apex seals (IK 3 special case-hardened castings). The inlet and exhaust were peripherally situated and petrol was fed into the inlet by a Bosch fuel injection pump. Two surface ignition type spark plugs for each combustion chamber were provided, using a transistorized ignition system.

This Wankel engine with all its accessories weighed approximately 3 cwt. With a compression ratio of 9,3:1 it delivered 280 bhp at 7000 rpm. Maximum torque of 217 lb.ft. was available between 5000 and 6500 rpm. A single plate clutch transmitted power to a five speed synchromesh ZF gearbox with limited slip differential. Because transmission was not an issue on this experimental vehicle, it was deemed preferable to use a well tried gear box rather than to develop a special new unit.

As speeds of about 170 mph were envisaged, four ventilated disc brakes were fitted to the car. Even higher performance appeared to be within reach because the engine department was busy developing a four-rotor Wankel unit. Therefore the C 111 was initially designed to accomodate the larger engine later.

The plastic body was built under the auspices of a body designer from the Sindelfingen works at the Rastätter Waggonfabrik. However, the development engineers could not wait for the first plastic body shell. As soon as the first chassis was available, an aluminium body was hurriedly produced for this prototype, without consideration for elegance or aerodynamics. It was merely to provide protection against wind and weather for the two test drivers.

On April 1 1969, the C 111 prototype went on its maiden voyage on the Daimler-Benz test track at Stuttgart-Unterturkheim. The first outing, quite naturally, led to a number of modifications. The first test drive on public roads was shared by Rudolf Uhlenhaut and C 111 project manager, Dr. Hans Liebold on April 16. On May 2, the prototype was taken to Hockenheim for the first time, and regular testing there as well as at Nürburgring continued for the rest of the month.

Weather conditions were good and the two technicians, both first rate drivers, took turns at the wheel for hours on end, exchanging opinions and finding the right suspension setting. It will be remembered that Rudolf Uhlenhaut was reserve driver in the Grand Prix team before and after World War Two, always lapping as fast as the best professional Formula One drivers.

Performance lived up to the high expectations, but the semi-trailing arm rear axle was hardly suited for a vehicle of this kind when equipped with the wide racing tyres that provided little flexibility against lateral forces. Directional stability was unsatisfactory, and there were considerable reactions under load changes in fast bends. Harder springs and dampers could have corrected this, but this was only acceptable on a pure racing car. For a road going Grand Tourer designed as a mobile test bed for production models, clearly an entirely different solution would have to be found. A rear suspension patterned after modern Grand Prix cars with transverse links and radius arms was therefore designed to attain an acceptable standard of comfort as well as satisfactory handling when driving the car to its limits. This offered the added advantage of permitting track and camber to be adjusted independently.

This result did not come quite so unexpectedly, and the rear suspension problem was the underlying reason the test drives with the prototype and its provisional alloy body were done in such a hurry. The decision to adopt the Grand Prix-type rear suspension was taken without delay, permitting the next batch of five cars to be so equipped from the beginning. The radius arms were designed to give an anti-dive effect as well.

Those five 'Series 1' cars were fitted with plastic bodies. For added rigidity, these were riveted and bonded onto the body platform. The C 111 body was fully equipped, with an elaborate heating and ventilation system, good sound and heat insulation, and a great many dashboard instruments. The interior was very luxurious. The first car was ready for the road on July 15 and it was immediately sent to Hockenheim for testing. The new rear suspension proved to be an excellent solution.

The other cars were all completed by the end of August and they were submitted to a long endurance programme. From September 1 to 15, at the time of the Frankfurt motor show, a series of demonstration drives was arranged for the press, technicians, and VIPs at Hockenheim.

The endurance tests took place on public roads, motorways, as well as on the Hockenheim and Nürburgring racing circuits. On the road, Michelin XVR radials were used, while conventional Dunlop racing tyres were fitted for the circuits. Throughout these tests, the cars were checked regularly and dismantled and modified whenever necessary. For example, the gear shift mechanism was redesigned and an electric switch installed to prevent inadvertent use of first or reverse gear. Also, the original single plate clutch with its long pedal travel for ease of operation, was replaced by a double plate clutch. The decreased clutch pressure thus achieved allowed a lower ratio to be used.

The C 111 Series 1 totalled six cars including the prototype. The last Series 1 car was the fifth with a plastic body. It differed from the others by weighing slightly less — and by being the first car to receive the four-rotor engine.

The C 111 with its three-rotor Wankel engine was undoubtedly a very fast car. Its top speed was about 170 mph, and acceleration of five seconds from standstill to 100 kph (62 mph) was claimed. This, however, seemed slightly optimistic, nevertheless there was hardly a rival to the C 111 on the German Autobahn. Yet it lacked something — a certain punch. An output of 280 bhp was developed at 7000 rpm from its overall chamber volume of 1800 cc (equivalent to 3600 cc in a reciprocating piston engine). This is 155,5 bhp per litre of chamber volume, a very high specific output for a Wankel engine even today. (The NSU Ro80, then in series production, achieved 115 bhp per litre, and the current emission controlled Mazda RX-7 delivers only 91 bhp per litre.) On the other hand, maximum torque of 217 lb.ft. only became available at 5000 rpm. Below 4500 rpm, acceleration left something to be desired for an ambitious car design like the C 111. At racing speed on a circuit, the C 111 acquitted itself well, although as a road going car it would not be competitive against sports racing cars. In a genuine Grand Touring car, one expects a certain amount of engine flexibility and low speed torque to go with outright performance. It is neither pleasant for the driver nor for the environment if the engine has to be kept at high revs. by constant gear changes — not to speak of the resulting high petrol consumption. When overtaking on the Autobahn one sometimes had the feeling that acceleration did not quite match the visual impact of the car. This, however, changed when the four-rotor engine was installed.

The bigger engine was far more flexible, not only because torque had increased by 33 percent to 288,5 lb.ft., (matching the increase in chamber volume to 2400 cc) but also because maximum torque was now available between 4000 and 5500 rpm, 1500 rpm lower than on the three-rotor unit. This was achieved at the expense of a slight reduction in specific output, down to 149 bhp per litre of chamber volume. But 350 bhp (at 7000 rpm) with a better low-speed torque was nevertheless satisfactory. The four-rotor C 111, now known as C 111-II, had a power to weight ratio of 8 lb. per bhp, and on the public roads it really could take on anything with wheels. The engine alone weighed only 3,5 cwt, giving a power to weight ratio of 1,1 lb. per bhp. Apart from the additional rotor and its internally moving parts, the lengthened eccentric shaft (running on five main bearings instead of four) and a different Bosch injection pump, the bigger engine was very much like its predecessor. Its length had grown by 6 in., and increased torque now made the double plate clutch essential.

Meanwhile the vehicle itself was being developed. A complete, road-ready C 111 was wind tunnel tested to improve its shape still further. The air intake for the radiator, originally positioned at headlight level, was moved to the tip of the nose and consequently lowered. Air outlets were provided on top of the bonnet in the low pressure zone. At high speeds aerodynamic downforce on the front axle could be increased by 20 percent.

During test drives on public roads, rear vision was unsatisfactory. Every effort was made to improve this. The side windows were extended rearwards, and the car's waistline was lowered. Finally, the rear fin shutters, so important for drag reduction, were abandoned, and only the frame retained. Reshaping the shutters for the original optimum effect required extensive wind tunnel testing. Furthermore, the boot above the gearbox, at the extreme rear, could be considerably enlarged with a complete redesign of the exhaust system. At the outset, two transverse silencers were situated above the gearbox. They were now installed longitudinally. The size of the luggage compartment was thus increased to an acceptable volume of nearly 9 cu.ft. Furthermore, it no longer heated up so badly. And when Rudolf Uhlenhaut had a small cooling fan installed, you could even transport butter in the luggage compartment.

The well finished plastic dashboard was also lowered for better forward visibility. Despite all these aesthetic and practical improvements it was possible to lower the drag coefficient yet again, to a C_R ratio of 0,325 for the C 111-II. The interior was revised, and sound and heat insulation further improved. The retractable headlights were now electrically operated, as foot operation had been found inconvenient at high speeds. All these improvements and the bigger engine made the C 111-II only 65 lb. heavier than the three-rotor version. With both aluminium tanks in the door sills carrying a total of 26 gallons of petrol, the total weight was now 26 cwt.

For this version, Mercedes announced a top speed of 187 mph (as timed by Dr. Liebold), as well as a time of 4,8 seconds from standstill to 100 kph (62 mph). There were no doubts about this figure now. Developing the C 111-I into the C 111-II was done with great vigour and tremendous enthusiasm. By the end of 1969, only five months after the first three-rotor vehicle with its final body had been completed, the first car with a four-rotor engine and the new body was ready for the road. In March 1970, it was officially revealed to the public at the Geneva show. The motoring press which had had some slight reservations about the first version of the C 111, enthusiastically received the C 111-II. Soon the public clamoured for the C 111-II to be built as a successor to the unforgettable 300 SL. Firm orders for such a vehicle, accompanied by blank cheques came in from various parts of the world. Members of the Daimler-Benz board certainly discussed the possibility of building a small series for sale to the public, but they finally decided against the move. There were still doubts about the relative reliability and durability of the Wankel engine. But Wankel development continued, and when Daimler-Benz was finally satisfied with the Wankel engine's behaviour in all these respects, the oil crisis of 1973 intervened. Furthermore anti-pollution legislation in many countries had become so strict that the Wankel engine no longer looked like a viable alternative.

FROM WANKEL TO DIESEL

The Diesel engine, however, had meanwhile gained much more importance. The world had grown increasingly energy conscious, and oil price increases made the very economical Diesel engine more likely even for the high end of the Mercedes range where top performance was taken for granted. Such considerations led to the development of the five-cylinder three-litre Diesel engine at Daimler-Benz. When it was launched, it was the most powerful Diesel engine offered in any car on the market. Fitted with a turbocharger, this engine was even destined to go into the S-class bodies for the American market. Yet many motorists were still sceptical of the Diesel. For them, a Diesel engined car, no matter how large or sophisticated, would always remain a lame duck. For an upmarket Diesel car to be sold in sufficiently large numbers, those sceptics would have to be convinced that a Diesel could be fast. Why could not the C 111 be used to prove that point? Such a project would, at the same time, give development engineers the chance to explore the limits of the Diesel engine.

So the first of the C 111-II cars, No. 31, was brought out of retirement. The big question was, however, how to use the car for optimum results. There were no racing events for Diesel engined cars, not even special classifications for Diesels, and in a scratch race against comparable petrol engined racing cars the Diesel would not stand a chance. Besides, the C 111 was no racing car. From the very beginning its concept had been that of a luxuriously appointed Grand Touring car. Therefore, it was not really fit for circuit racing, nor for modern rallies, regardless of the engine used. But the engineers knew that the output of the current, standard five-cylinder Diesel of 80 bhp could easily be more than doubled with the aid of a turbocharger, without detrimental effect on its reliability. One hundred and ninety bhp could certainly be obtained, and that would mean the fastest Diesel the world had ever seen. Such a vehicle should be able to wipe out all the existing long distance records for Diesel cars. The venue for such a record attempt then became the next big question. A circuit would have to be found in Europe which allowed full use of the car's potential speed — over 155 mph — for hours on end. Luckily, SNIA, a Fiat subsidiary, had recently built a high speed circular test track at Nardo, near Lecce, in Southern Italy. This 7,8 mile circuit with its banked curves of 13 degrees was designed to allow a theoretical speed of 150 mph where no side forces would act on the car. At that speed, a car could be driven round the circuit with hands off. The Diesel record car could therefore be fully exploited on this track with practically no side forces, and with hardly any of the lateral slip which increases rolling resistance. For such a record attempt it mattered little that the car was relatively heavy. It was only necessary to accelerate the car once at the start and once after every pit stop. Otherwise it would run at constant speed. The small additional rolling resistance played an insignificant part in the total tractive resistance, because the predominant component at such high speeds is aerodynamic drag.

As soon as these problems had been sorted out satisfactorily, the Board of Directors approved the record attempts. All medium and long distance Diesel records in the two to three litre class were to be tackled, and Dr. Liebold was put in charge of the project.

Replacing the Wankel engine by a Diesel unit presented no major problem as the five-cylindre engine was relatively short, and also a bit narrower than the Wankel unit. Also, the bulky and heat-emanating silencers could be dispensed with. The engine itself was close to standard. The main bearings used for the record car's engine were later adopted on the standard production Diesel Turbo. In addition to the standard sodium-cooled exhaust valves, sodium cooling was used on the inlet valves. The pistons were lowered slightly to reduce the compression ratio. Also, the bore was narrowed by 0,1 mm to bring engine displacement within the three litre class limit from the 3005 cc capacity of the standard 300 D model. The standard oil sump was replaced by a bigger and flatter one.

The type T-04B Garrett turbocharger gave a boost pressure of 26,5 lb./sq.in. It was adapted to the engine in such a way as to require no pressure regulator valve. Such a solution is only acceptable when torque at lower and medium revs is unimportant. On the other hand, it gives optimum efficiency. Air was fed to the engine by a large air cooled charge air cooler. The Bosch fuel injection pump automatically adjusted the amount of fuel relative to boost pressure, a system later adopted for the standard Mercedes Turbo Diesel models. As maximum engine revolutions (maximum output of 190 bhp at 4200 to 4700 rpm) were considerably lower than on the Wankel, gearbox ratios had to be altered. The overall ratio of 5th gear now became 2,17:1.

The long distances of the planned record attempts made day and night driving necessary. Consequently, headlights were required, but for aerodynamic reasons retractable headlights were out of question. On the roadgoing version these were indispensable to meet legal requirements for minimum headlight height. With the retractable headlights down, the C 111 showed a drag coefficient of about $C_R = 0,3$, an excellent value for a road car. Drag increased considerably, however, when the headlights were up. Therefore the retractable system was abandoned on the record car, and the headlights were fitted into the mudguards under a Plexiglass cover. Additional spotlights were installed in the front air intakes.

Tyre selection led to an interesting decision. Radial tyres have less rolling resistance than conventional cross-ply tyres. In principle, they also show less wear, although this depends a lot on the rubber. Racing tyres have much narrower characteristics than road tyres. A racing tyre designed for use on a dry track offers dangerously little grip on a wet track, while rain tyres heat up when run on a dry road and could throw a tread. The best solution seemed the use of the Michelin XVR high speed radial road tyre (forerunner of today's XWX) which allowed sustained speeds of 160 mph with higher tyre pressures. It showed little wear and could be used in the rain as well as on a dry track. Apart from that, it excelled by giving very low rolling resistance.

The two fuel tanks in the door sills were enlarged to hold 15,5 gallons each which gave a range of 2,5 hours. In the interest of aerodynamics, unventilated disc brakes were used. Brake cooling was unimportant because the brakes were only used before pit stops.

Pit stops were also practiced during extensive test drives. After training, refuelling only took eight to 10 seconds. The record attempt was then started on June 12 1976. The drivers selected all came from the Daimler-Benz experimental department. They were Dr. Hans Liebold (C 111 project manager, who had also done all the test driving), Joachim Kaaden, Erich Waxenberger (in charge of motor sport development), and Guido Moch (in charge of test driving at Untertürkheim). This team drove for 60 hours, with driver changes every 2,5 hours. Weather remained good, and all existing international class records in the up to three litre Diesel class for distances from 10 kilometres to 10 000 miles were wiped out. In most cases they were improved by at least 37 mph. The records for 5000 miles, 10 000 km, and 10 000 miles also counted as world records irrespective of cubic capacity limits. The list below shows that all records except those over 10 km and 10 miles were at more than 155 mph. This is because the mandatory standing start has a greater effect on the average speed for the shortest distances.

C 111-II Diesel record runs at the Nardo track, 1976 International Class records for Diesel up to 3000 cc (World records irrespective of class are marked*)

10 km	137,030 mph	1000 km	157,334 mph
10 miles	141,213 mph	1000 miles	156,980 mph
100 km	155,993 mph	5000 km	157,083 mph
100 miles	157,127 mph	5000 miles	156,857 mph*
500 km	157,817 mph	10 000 km	156,676 mph*
500 miles	157,099 mph	10 000 miles	156,396 mph*
1 hour	157,621 mph	12 hours	157,525 mph
6 hours	156,880 mph	24 hours	157,161 mph

The highest record speed was attained over the first 500 kilometres — the distance before the first fuel stop. The most impressive however, were the world records for 10 000 km and 10 000 miles, with speeds of more than 156 mph. Nobody could claim any longer that Diesel cars were lame ducks. The car's impressive performance was further substantiated when, during trial runs using suitable gear ratios, it reached 100 kph (62 mph) from a standing start in only 6,8 seconds.

C 111-III: A TRUE RECORD-BREAKER

Impressive as they were, the new records left the engineers from Daimler-Benz with a bitter taste. The C 111-II was a vehicle designed and developed for road use, with all the legal and practical limitations that this entailes. The car was a comfortable and spacious two-seater which meant a fairly large frontal area. For practical purposes the front and rear overhang of the body were kept short — particularly at the rear — and aerodynamic compromises had to be accepted to ensure certain minimum standards of rear vision. Technicians and mechanics were sulking: "Had we been permitted to build a true record breaking vehicle, we'd be close to the 300 kph limit (186 mph) by now". Professor Hans Scherenberg, technical director on the Board of Daimler-Benz, became the spokesman of that opinion. He was the man who had put all his energy into the development of the five-cylinder Diesel engine. As an individual he was friendly, soft-spoken, almost shy, but very convincing in his arguments. On the Board of Directors he proposed that the C 111 Project should be extended towards further record attempts — and his colleagues on the Board fully accepted his views. By early 1977 the styling department at Sindelfingen began to produce drawings and Plasticine models from data provided by the experimental department. The existing body platform was to be retained but in the interests of a sleeker body, the wheelbase was increased by 4 in. to 107 in. On the other hand, track had to be narrowed to obtain a smaller frontal area. Front track was reduced by 6 in. to 50 in., while rear track could only be narrowed by 4 in. to 52 in. A further reduction was deemed unwise in view of drive shaft stresses.

Great efforts were made to keep body and windscreen as narrow as possible. However, consideration had to be given to the very comprehensive dashboard instruments, to the pipes running through the cockpit (particularly a large diameter tube feeding cooling air to the charge air cooler), to the radio and finally to driver comfort, so important on long distance record runs. On the other hand, rear vision could be totally ignored, which greatly facilitated aerodynamic development.

The most promising designs were then built as 1:5 scale models for testing in a small laboratory wind tunnel. Smoke was used to make airflow visible, and to determine areas of turbulence. In this manner, the model finally selected could be further improved and modified before making a full scale clay model. The numerous air intakes and outlets were then scooped out of the full scale model and connected with air ducts where required, in preparation for full scale airflow tests in the large wind tunnel. The intake and outlet openings were not only shaped for optimum airflow through the car but to prevent aerodynamic loss. The air ducts' cross sections could be kept smaller if the pressure difference between intake and outlet was greater. This meant reduced drag.

Yet the drag coefficient is not the only important aerodynamic aspect on such a car. Aerodynamic lift or downforce at the front and rear axle are also very important, as is cross wind sensitivity. All these factors have to be considered in wind tunnel tests. Developing a car aerodynamically in wind tunnel tests means long experiments with continuous alternations and adjustments to the rake of the nose, the front spoilers and rear wings, until the optimum overall effect has been obtained.

From the full scale clay model, a negative was then formed to make the mould for production of the definitive body shell at the Rastätter Waggonfabrik. It was important to achieve a sufficiently rigid body surface which would maintain its optimum shape, while submitted to strong air pressures at high speeds. The material used was highly resistant polyester resin, reinforced by glass-fibre and carbon-fibre mats. Points of high stress were further strengthened by boron-fibre tapes 0,75 in. thick, a technique previously employed only in the aircraft industry. The overall weight of the complete body was only 4 cwt. Despite the very rigid body structure, the long rear end needed additional support in the form of a tubular aluminium framework.

After the long distance record runs with the C 111-II Diesel, the engine was stripped and thoroughly checked. The engineers concluded from the engine's first class condition that 190 bhp was by no means the maximum performance obtainable from this power unit. Output was therefore raised, and endurance bench tests confirmed the engine's reliability under these new conditions. Piston cooling was improved with the aid of larger oil injector nozzles. Additional power was mainly the result of altered inlet cams (longer valve opening time) and a higher boost pressure of 31 lb./sq.in. This led to a reduction in the compression ratio to 17,5:1, and gas flow was improved by reducing the valve seat angle to 20 degrees. The resultant output was just over 230 bhp at 4200 to 4600 rpm, and maximum torque was increased to 296,5 lb.ft. at 3700 rpm. Under these conditions the Garrett turbocharger operated at 130 000 rpm. The large charge air cooler was configured to reduce the temperature of compressed air from about 350°F to 175°F.

In view of the more powerful engine and the greatly reduced drag compared with the C 111-II, the overall ratio of 5th gear was reduced to 1,65:1, corresponding with a road speed of 44,7 mph at 1000 rpm.

Suspension remained essentially unchanged from previous C 111 versions.

However, at the expected sustained speeds far surpassing 300 kph (186 mph) road tyres had to be ruled out, especially in consideration of the resultant lateral acceleration of 0,2 g., despite the bank of 13 degrees. After several test drives it was decided to use Dunlop diagonal racing tyres especially developed for these record attempts. They were fitted to wheels of 15 in. x 8 in. (front) and 15 in. x 9,5 in. (rear). The springs had to be adapted to the lateral accelerations as well. Slightly longer springs had to be fitted on the outside in order to maintain the car on a parallel course under lateral forces at high speeds. The wheels were equipped with central lock in view of the numerous tyre changes expected.

A two way radio communications system between driver and pit crew was provided. The pilot could establish radio contact with the pits by pressing a button on a spoke of the steering wheel. An entirely new development was the automatic telemetric transmission of the most important engine data to the pits each time the car passed the starting line. Apart from the official time keeping by the sporting authorities, the car was automatically timed on each lap with the aid of an electronic beacon, and a calculator automatically computed lap time, lap speed, and overall average speed. This system was developed by Daimler-Benz. The record car turned the scales at 24 cwt (with full tanks). Yet another 150 lb. of necessary spare parts had to be carried on board to meet the international sporting code for record attempts. Thus, the C 111-III with driver on board weighed a maximum 27 cwt.

Before the record attempts, the car was sent to Nardo twice for preliminary tests. These mainly involved tyre testing, experiments with certain aerodynamic variations, and setting up the suspension as well as the aerodynamic aids (spoilers etc.) of the car. Meanwhile a second car, built to the latest specifications, was destined to be the actual vehicle for the record attempt. On the last few days before the record runs, on April 30 1978, both cars were finally prepared taking into account the weather conditions then prevailing in Southern Italy. The three wide, frontal air intakes proved to be superfluous, and covering them up added another 2,5 mph to the lap speeds. Wind tunnel measurements of the actual record-breaking vehicle gave a drag coefficient of $C_R = 0,183$ — probably a world record in itself. With a frontal area of 15,8 sq.ft. this gave C_R x F = 2,9 sq.ft., less than one third of the drag of an average saloon.

Finally, a new engine was installed in the spare car to render it fully operational just in case something went wrong during the record attempt. This time, all records up to and including 12 hours were to be attacked. Drivers were Guido Moch, (47), ex-racing driver Rico Steinemann (38, now PR manager of Mercedes-Benz, Switzerland), and this writer Paul Frère (61, motoring journalist and former Grand Prix driver).

A few hours before the start, some mechanics did one lap of the track on foot, collecting any litter that could possibly cause tyre damage. Their outing was successful indeed, for they came back with a box full of all kinds of nuts and bolts and other metal parts lost by the many cars that were constantly tested at the Nardo track.

Just before midnight, April 29 1978, Paul Frère set out for a warming up lap under a dark blue, star-lit sky. Then the right-hand fuel tank was topped up and the record attempt was started precisely at zero hours on April 30 1978. The record runs were directed by Professor Werner Breitschwert, the new Board member for research and development, successor to Professor Scherenberg who had reached retirement age. For safety reasons the record runs were done in an anti-clockwise direction. The pilot was therefore on the inside of the curve, as the car had left hand steering.

The extra long final drive ratio meant that it took the C 111-III about one lap (7,86 miles) to reach its top speed. On about the third lap, the speed stabilized at about 202 mph, with fluctuations of less than 1 mph from lap to lap.

The two way radio proved extremely useful, reducing the pilot's fatigue by breaking the monotony of the 2,5-hour driving spells. More important still, any irregularity could be reported back to the pits immediately. After about 10 laps, I noticed a hedgehog sitting on the left of the lane I was using. Had it crossed my path, I would have hit it, demolishing both the hedgehog and the front spoiler. I reported the hedgehog's exact position to the pits by radio, and it was duly removed by the pit staff before an incident arose.

Thanks to the two 100 Watt HELLA halogen headlights, night driving presented no problems. I even had time to read the various instruments — 13 in all — at regular intervals and to report the most important data to the pits, as a double check against the telemetrically transmitted data.

The very direct Daimler-Benz recirculating ball steering was a bit on the heavy side, but this was accepted because at such speeds, instant and precise response is vital in an emergency. Besides, there are no tight corners to negotiate during record runs, and the car was so stable directionally that steering corrections were hardly ever necessary. However, a certain amount of left lock was constantly required to counterbalance the side force of 500 lb. acting on the car. Interior ventilation was rather good, so the 2,5-hour driving session at an average speed of over 199 mph was far less tiring than expected. Sixty two laps or 288 miles were covered non-stop. Driver morale received boosts every now and then when the pits reported by radio: "You have just broken the 100 km world record", and soon after, "now you have the 100 miles world record in the bag". A little later, news came that the one hour world record, and then, that the 500 km world record had been broken.

Preparations for the pit stop required full concentration. The record car, as with most racing cars, has no power brakes. Even when applying the highest possible pedal pressure it takes an awfully long time to bring the speed down from 200 mph. The extremely low drag of the C 111-III meant that the air provided only one third of the braking effect of a normal saloon. Radio instructions were comprehensive and precise: "Advise pits when car passes between the eight and 9 km signs; take off seat belt and attach to hook positioned on tube of charge air cooler; switch back to right hand petrol tank (which was always emptied first for better weight distribution); step off accelerator pedal when passing the 11 km sign and apply brakes gently". At the same time, to save the brakes, one had to change down; but this had to be done very carefully, so as not to overrev the engine, as the gaps between gearbox ratios were quite large. These careful preparations were important because the slightest omission or mistake would render the driver change longer than the 15 seconds refuelling time. At every stop, about one pint of engine oil was added.

Later that night we were faced with fog that grew thicker and thicker. Guido Moch was at the wheel, pressing on very courageously, using the guardrail as an optical guide line and keeping his foot firmly on the floor. Then Rico Steinemann took over and we all became more and more optimistic. Then, all of a sudden, there was silence... Steinemann had thrown a tread of the right hand rear tyre, possibly the result of an earlier loss of tyre pressure. The tyre disintegrated, ripping off a large chunk of the body. Steinemann very ably managed to keep the car on the track but it was too badly damaged to continue the record run.

Immediately the spare car was taken out and the record attempt started anew. To ease the task of the drivers, project manager Hans Liebold, who had done all the preliminary testing, took the wheel immediately. The spare car proved fractionally faster than the first one, and all the world records set up the previous day were again broken by a few decimals. Furthermore, the spare car was more economical which increased driving spells between pit stops to 67 laps. Thus, the 500 mile world record could be driven non-stop, and completed before the first refuelling was due. For an interesting reason, the 500 mile record speed was marginally lower than the one for 500 km. Fuel began to warm up, and its density decreased as a result. The fastest laps were always the ten laps after a fuel stop, when speeds of about 203 mph were attained, corresponding with 4550 rpm. Then the car became gradually slower until the last laps before refuelling when it could reach only 198 to 199 mph. During the night there was another incident. Rico Steinemann was at the wheel again, and his bad luck continued. He ran over a hedgehog and damaged the front spoiler which cost a two minute pit stop for replacement.

No other problems arose and after 12 hours, Daimler-Benz was richer by nine world records. It should be noted that world records (as distinct from international class records) are always irrespective of engine system or cubic capacity limits. These world records are therefore all the more remarkable as they were established by a Diesel engine fairly close to standard production, and with a capacity of only three litres. The following world records were set up:

100 km	196,574 mph	1 hour	199,902 mph
100 miles	198,655 mph	6 hours	197,389 mph
500 km	199,913 mph	12 hours	195,319 mph
500 miles	199,247 mph		
1000 km	197,707 mph		
1000 miles	198,193 mph		

The fastest lap during the record run was at 203,3 mph. The most remarkable achievement during the record attempts, however, will never feature in the official list of records. The C 111-III showed an oustandingly low fuel consumption of 17,6 mpg during the entire record run at an average speed of just under 200 mph. This, perhaps, is the most interesting conclusion of these Diesel record runs. It only goes to show how much can be achieved in the realm of fuel economy when engine efficiency and aerodynamic development reach an optimum.

250 MPH BREAKTHROUGH

In 1975, the late Mark Donohue, prominent American racing driver, set a record unrecognised by the FIA. Driving a CanAm Porsche 917/30 with more than 1000 bhp under the bonnet, he lapped the 6,2 mile oval race track of Talladega, Alabama in the United States at 221,027 mph, faster than any man had lapped any circuit. This constituted the so-called circuit world record. After the successful C 111-III record runs, Daimler-Benz eagerly looked at this coveted, though unofficial record. To the technicians it seemed within reach. The C 111-III could have beaten it with another 100 bhp under the bonnet. The almost standard Turbo Diesel engine could not, of course, be made to produce that extra power. Turbocharging a near standard V8 petrol engine would be the obvious answer. A 450 engine as used in the S-class as well as in the SL/SLC models was selected for the exercise. This engine was bored out to 4,8 litres and fitted with two KKK turbochargers. As on the Diesel, the turbochargers were adjusted to make maximum boost pressure coincide with maximum power revolutions. Thereby a pressure regulator valve could be avoided and the turbochargers would operate with optimum efficiency. Flatter pistons were used to lower the engine compression ratio. As on the Diesel, sodium-cooled valves were fitted. This resulted in a solid 500 bhp at 6200 rpm with good reliability. Despite the much higher road speeds envisaged, higher engine revolutions required a change in the overall ratio of the 5th gear from 1,65 to 1,82. Higher torque — 441 lb.ft. at 5250 rpm — meant replacing the double plate clutch by a triple plate one. Lateral acceleration with the C 111-III had been just under 0,2 g, but on the C 111-IV, as the new car was designated, it would be 0,4 g. The effect of the track's banking would be to press the car against the ground with a side force of about 450 lb, raising overall wheel load to 3500 lb. Two problems resulted from this, both providing headaches for the development engineers: tyres and aerodynamics. The C 111-III was drivable with a relatively small downforce. At the rear axle, the car was even submitted to some lift. With lateral acceleration of 0,4 g as expected on the C 111-IV, a much greater downforce was essential for directional control.

Yet ideally, this aerodynamic downforce should, if possible, be obtained without deterioration of the drag coefficient. Greater downforce, however, also means additional tyre loads. Tyres, therefore, would present a much greater problem than on the C 111-III. The doubled lateral force would, result in much greater wear and heat build-up. Raising the speeds from 200 to 250 mph would mean a 60 percent increase in the centrifugal force acting on the tyre.

For directional control and to reduce cross wind sensitivity the C 111-IV was fitted with two rear fins, and greater downforce was obtained by front and rear spoilers just below wheel hub level. Positioning the rear spoiler at such a low level proved to be less detrimental to a good drag coefficient than fitting a wing between the rear fins. It should be noted that the spoilers were asymmetrical and designed to provide more downforce on the left than on the right hand side of the car. As the circuit was used in an anti-clockwise direction this was to balance out the rolling moment created by centrifugal force. The results were equal wheel loads left and right. At the same time, efforts were made to balance the drag increase resulting from the spoilers by further aerodynamic improvements of the body. Lengthening the rear end of the body and reshaping the front end resulted in considerable improvements which almost completely offset the drag effect of the new spoilers. In its definitive form the C 111-IV had a drag coefficient of C_R = 0,182. Paradoxically, the blunt and steeper front end of the C 111-IV was aerodynamically more favourable than the wedge shaped nose of the C 111-III (C_R = 0,183). This indicates that the C 111-III could have gone just a little bit faster with some further aerodynamic improvements.

The main objective of the C 111-IV was to break Donohue's unofficial circuit world record. Apart from that, short and medium distance records were aimed at. This made the task for the tyre manufacturer entirely different. Tyre wear was only a minor consideration but directional stability and above all, reliability, were absolutely vital. A tyre blow-out at 250 mph with lateral acceleration of 0,4 g meant that the driver would not stand a chance of maintaining control over his vehicle. A radial tyre specially developed and built for this project by Michelin was finally chosen. Even so, the French manufacturer would not guarantee these tyres at the speeds envisaged for more than 30 minutes.

Having passed all preliminary test runs during which suspension and aerodynamic aids were set up for optimum performance, the record attempt was fixed for May 5 1979. Project manager, Dr. Hans Liebold, who had done the test runs, would drive in the record attempt himself. No problems were encountered during the record runs, but Liebold soon found out that some small bumps on this otherwise excellent track caused such severe battering at the speed of the C 111-IV that they had to be avoided. For fast saloons, and even for the C 111-III, these bumps had been harmless, but the extra 50 mph made all the difference.

Mark Donohue's record established at the wheel of a Porsche 917/30 with more than twice the C 111-IV's power was improved by 30 mph. The new circuit world record was set at 250,918 mph. Within the 30 minutes allotted to the record run (for tyre reasons), four more world records were established:

| 10 km | 199,140 mph | 100 km | 233,335 mph |
| 10 miles | 207,114 mph | 100 miles | 228,196 mph |

These figures and results raise the question, whether such record attempts justify the efforts and expenses invested. Apart from the resultant publicity, what sense do they make? In other words, what is the benefit of such record runs for the average motorist? The same question may be raised in connection with Mercedes participation in international rallies, which has recently been increased.

It cannot be denied that the Diesel records have been excellent publicity for Diesel products. In the public mind they have removed a sales obstacle by establishing the opinion that Diesel engined cars not only save fuel, they can be very fast at the same time. But the development of record and rally cars is far more important for technical progress. Lightweight construction and aerodynamics will play a much more important rôle in automotive design during the years to come. Aerodynamics will have a double function, first to save fuel, and second to improve handling. This last function is all the more important as the cars of the future will be very much lighter than to-day. Developing record cars which go twice as fast as most normal saloons means using new material for lightweight construction. By submitting such vehicles and their components to extreme stresses, Daimler-Benz are amassing a lot of highly useful experience. This will find its use in series production cars of the future. In fact it will ensure that Daimler-Benz can maintain the leading position in car design which it holds today. This will remain true even if one day the criteria by which cars are judged may have changed. Daimler-Benz is prepared for this contingency.

FROM WANKEL TO DIESEL:
THE EVOLUTION OF THE C 111

It was the interest generated by the rotary Wankel engine in the automobile world of 1969 that instigated Daimler-Benz to build a high-performance, experimental car. The car was to allow Daimler-Benz to test new ideas in body construction and in plastics. It was thus that the first C 111 was born. For many years, the C 111 successfully fulfilled its role as a laboratory vehicle. It was later fitted with a four-rotor engine, and finally with a supercharged, five-cylinder Diesel unit to become the C 111-II. In 1979 it broke a series of records on the Nardo circuit.

Early in 1969, the team of technicians responsible for the project discussed the first plans for a high performance experimental car powered by a Wankel engine (from left to right): Sorsche van Winsen, Göschel, Uhlenhaut, Wilfert, Scherenberg, and Breitschwerd inspecting scale models of the body platform.

At Sindelfingen, Plasticine 1:5 scale models of the most promising designs were built for wind tunnel testing. The version finally selected was then produced as a full scale model for further development.

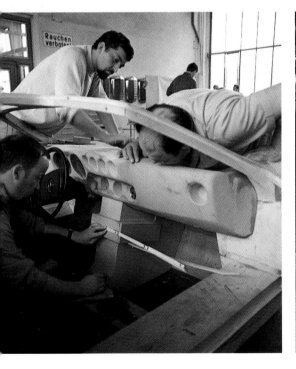

Top: Testing the 1:5 scale model in a small wind tunnel. Smoke makes the airflow visible.
Bottom: The completed prototype and (right hand page) the first C 111 in its definite form are tested in the big wind tunnel. Attached woolen threads show areas of turbulence.

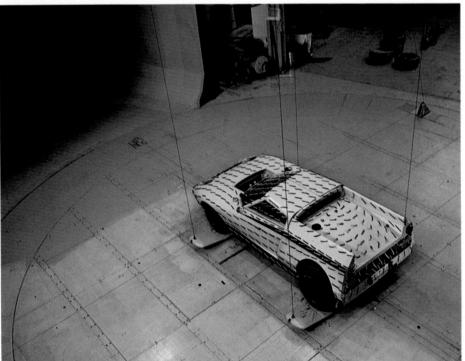

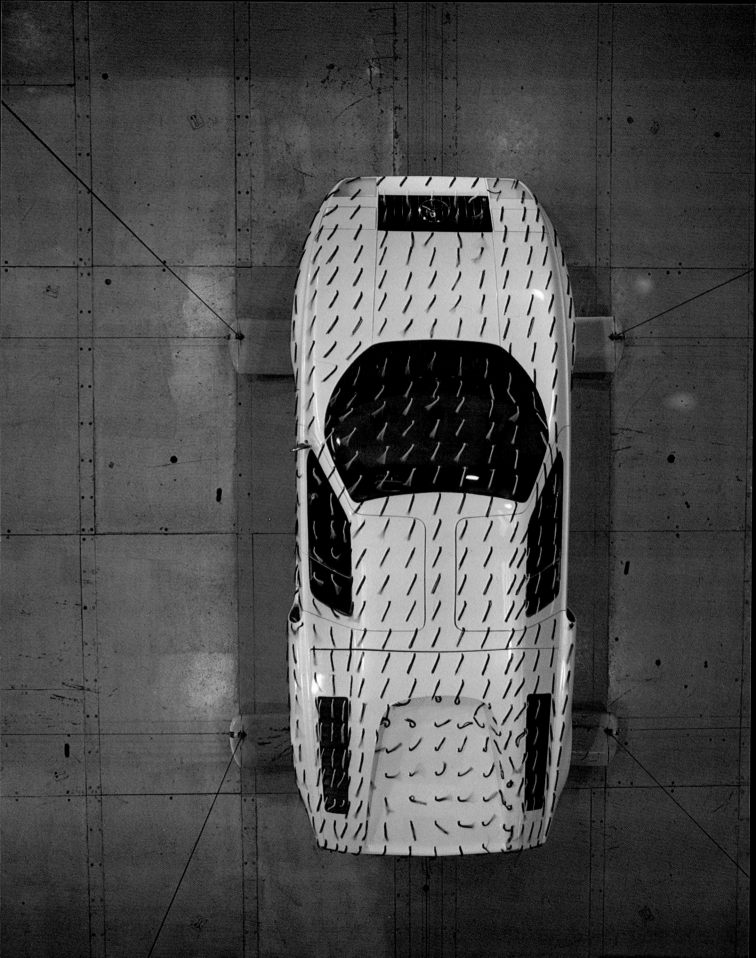

The full scale model in its ultimate form, before the first version of the C 111 was signed off by the board of directors.

The three-rotor Wankel engine seen through a rotor housing.

Dieter Bensinger, chief of engine design looks at one of the three rotors inside the trochoid. Bottom: A rotor inside the trochoid.

Two generations of high performance Daimler-Benz cars. Next to the legendary W 163 Grand Prix car of 1939, the first C 111 is being assembled.

To save valuable time, the prototype body was made of sheet aluminium. Its shape merely approximated the definite version. Here, a second, improved version of the body front with integrated headlights is being shaped.

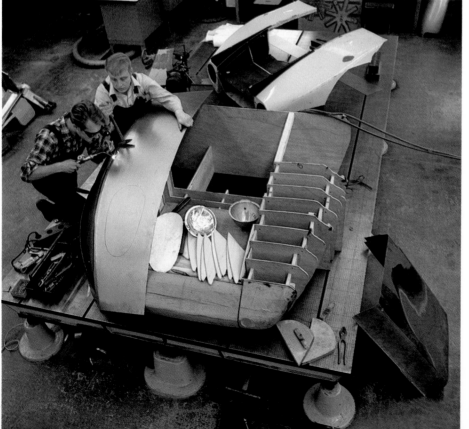

The prototype at full speed in the banked curve of the Daimler-Benz test track at Untertürkheim.

Rudolf Uhlenhaut (wearing crash helmet), chief of car development, and Hans Liebold, C 111 Project Manager, swap impressions after the first C 111 test drive at Hockenheim on April 1969. The prototype was fitted with the provisional aluminium body.

46

The first car out of the initial batch of five units was completed on July 15 1969. It was immediately sent to Hockenheim for extensive test drives.

Gull-wing doors and foot-operated, retractable headlights characterise the Series I version of the
C 111. Its air intakes were on top of the bonnet at headlight level. Its top speed was 168 mph.

The C 111 used Dunlop racing tyres (see photograph) on race tracks, while Michelin XVR tyres were fitted for road use. The gear box is by ZF.

The C 111, essentially an experimental car, was continually modified to try out new solutions.

Experience gained from the first version led to the C 111-II with a wheelbase lengthened to 103 ins. This four-inch increase allowed the installation of a four-rotor Wankel engine. Rear vision could also be improved and interior space enlarged. Modified cooling air ducts reduced aerodynamic lift.

The four-rotor Wankel engine developed 350 bhp, giving the C 111-II a top speed of 185 mph.

Three generations of the C 111: The prototype, a C 111-I, and a C 111-II. The latest version featured a lower waistline and cut out rear fins for better vision. The retractable headlights were electrically operated. Only the first C 111-II used a grille to protect the air intake (right).

The Diesel-engined C 111-II record-breaking car had no retractable headlights. Relatively narrow Michelin radial tyres were used to reduce rolling resistance.

In 1975, the four-rotor Wankel engine in one of the C 111-IIs was replaced by a turbocharged five-cylinder Diesel engine of 190 bhp. This car set a number of world records at distances of up to 10 000 miles and at speeds exceeding 155 mph on the Nardo circuit.

THE BIRTH OF THE C 111

In the beginning of 1977, the Daimler-Benz management decided to produce a true, record-breaking car. It was to be the C 111-III, powered by a turbocharged, five-cylinder Diesel engine.

It was obvious that these new Diesel records could be improved quite easily by pushing aerodynamic development a bit further. At Sindelfingen, some preparatory designs were prepared (left and following double page).

It was decided to build a genuine record car. The main dimensions were laid down by the technicians. Then the styling department prepared dozens of proposals, one of which is under scrutiny here by van Winsen, chief of car development, and Huber, car body development engineer.

Preparing various 1:5 scale models for
wind tunnel testing.

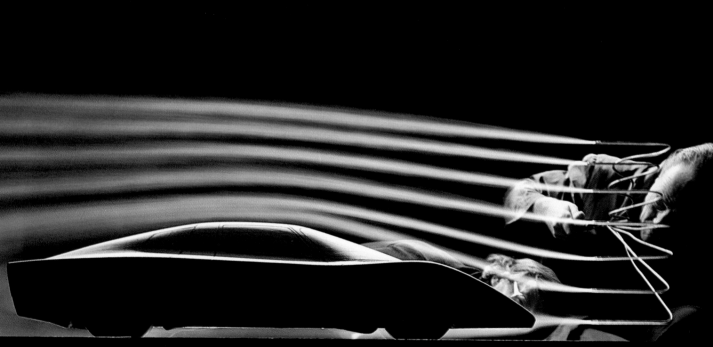

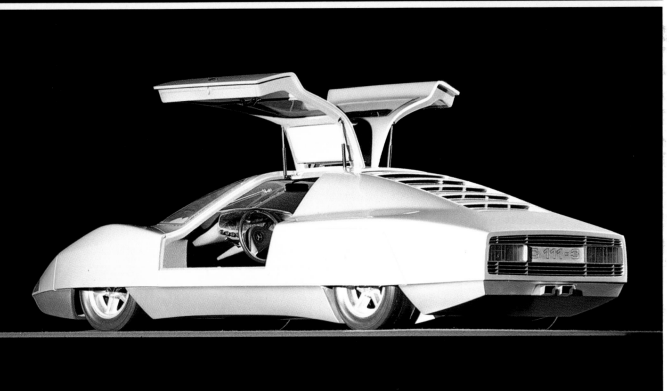

This 1:5 scale model closely approximates the final car. By reducing track and width, the car had a lower frontal area than its predecessor. It is considerably longer and shows a more fleeting body line.

The first completed car is ready for wind tunnel testing. As windscreen wipers create turbulence, they are only fitted when it rains.

Even the seats were first formed in Plasticine. The design shown here was not selected for production.

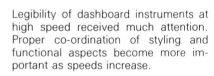

Legibility of dashboard instruments at high speed received much attention. Proper co-ordination of styling and functional aspects become more important as speeds increase.

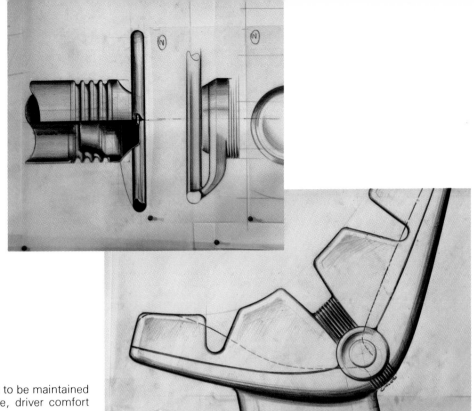

Speeds in excess of 185 mph will have to be maintained for hours in record attempts. Therefore, driver comfort comes high on the priority list.

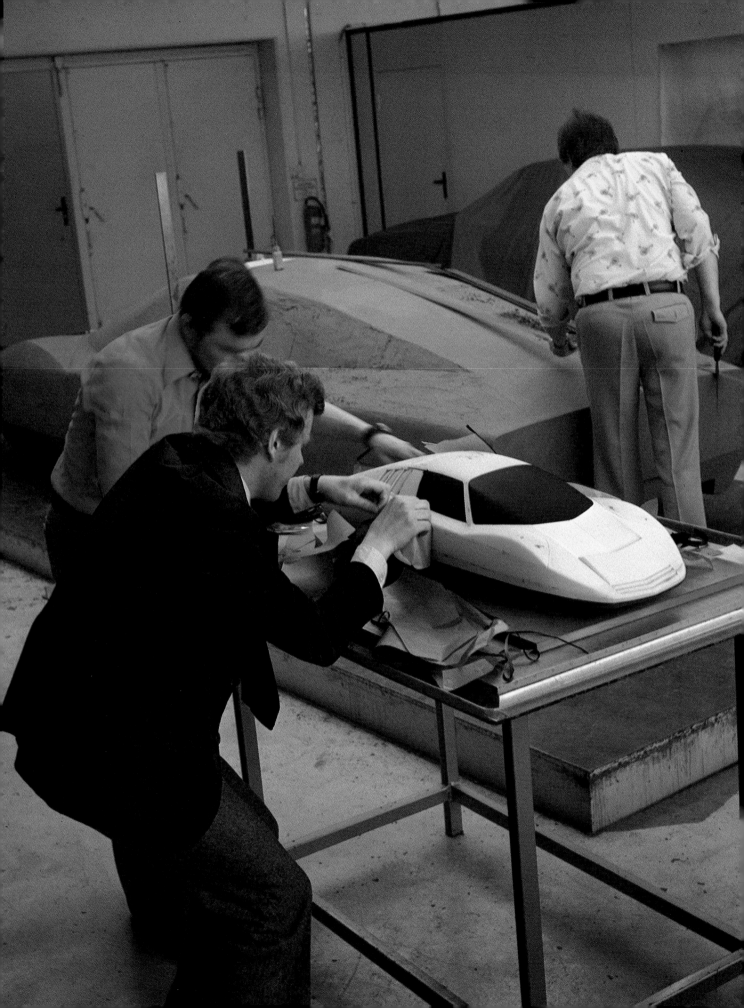

A 1:5 scale Plasticine model is measured and the resulting data serve to build a full scale clay model.

The completed clay model is electronically measured (top) and these data are automatically transferred on to paper to produce the definite drawings (bottom).

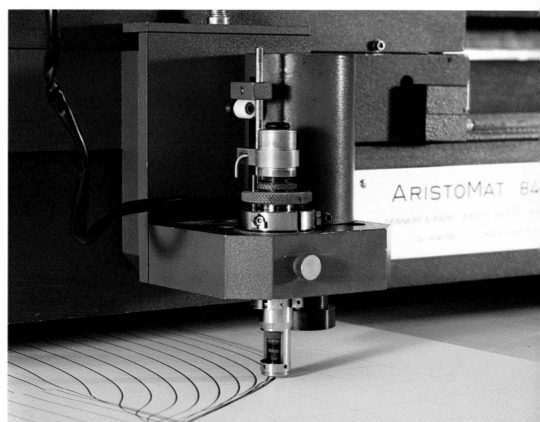

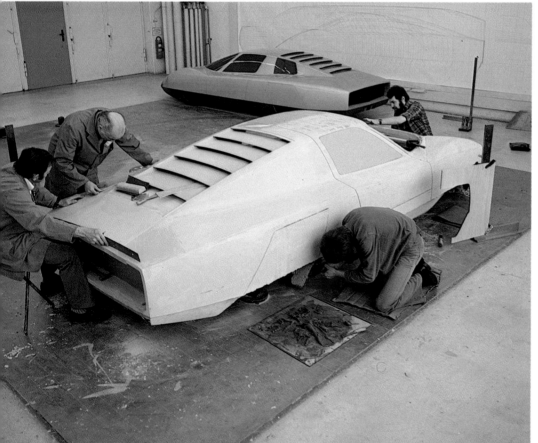

Integrating the mechanical parts into the clay model. The cockpit fully corresponds to that in the real car in its final form.

Putting finishing touches on the full scale clay model.

Covering the wheel arches can reduce drag considerably.

Air ducts are cut into the clay model to simulate the airflow inside the car during wind tunnel tests.

Straight, motionless, woolen threads
indicate good airflow. Right: Testing a
number of variations.

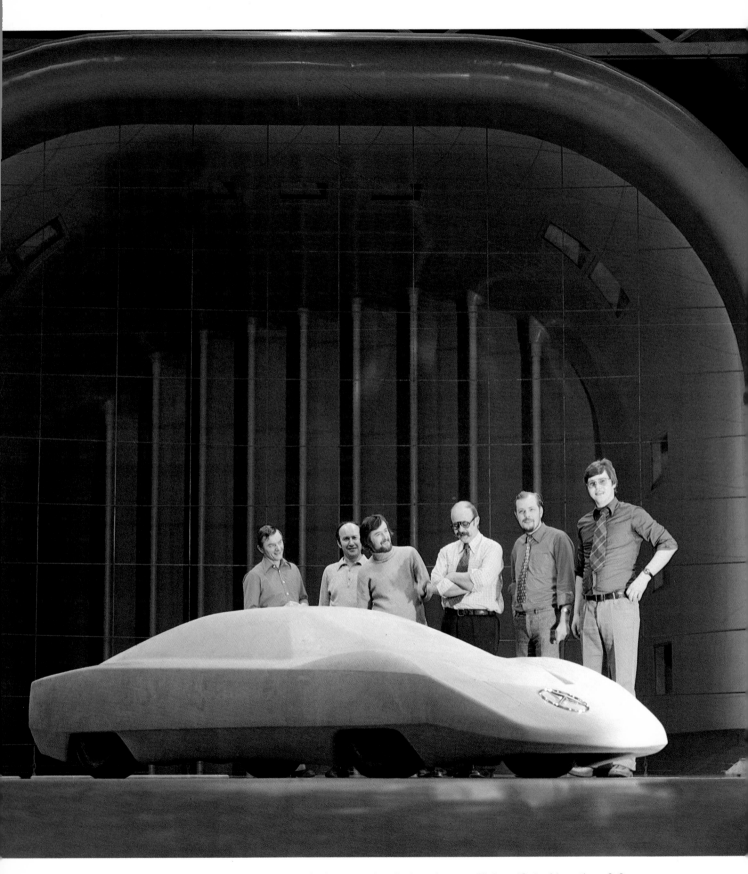

The team is well pleased with the exceptionally low drag coefficient (c_R) of less than 0,2.

THE MAKING OF THE C 111-III

It took less than a year to build the C 111-III after the Daimler-Benz management decision. The first trials took place at Nardo in the winter of 1977-1978.

The body platform is welded steel. In the interests of directional stability and sleeker body contours, the wheelbase was increased by four inches. The plastic body shell is bonded onto the steel framework.

Many man-hours and lots of balsa wood go into the construction of the negative mould for the body shell. On this matrix the plastic body, reinforced by glass-, carbon-, and boron-fibre, will be moulded.

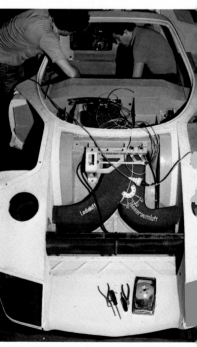

Building the plastic body at the Rastätter Waggonfabrik. On the left (top right), are Reinhard (chief of special constructions), Dieckmann (chief of car body design), Huber (present chief of car body development), and Haug, the plastics expert (far left).

The totally flat underfloor of the body, made of carbon-fibre-reinforced plastic contributed greatly to the low drag. The rear NACA air duct serves to ventilate the engine compartment.

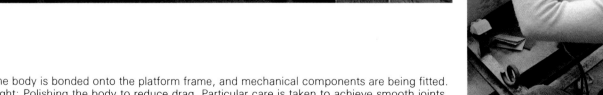

The body is bonded onto the platform frame, and mechanical components are being fitted. Right: Polishing the body to reduce drag. Particular care is taken to achieve smooth joints.

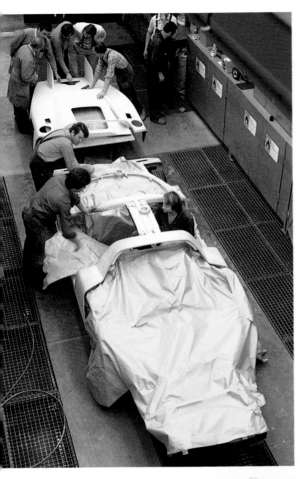

Painting and polishing the first completed body in the railway carriage assembly hall at the Rastätter Waggonfabrik. A perfectly smooth surface can contribute to the car's top speed.

The large rear end of the body weighs next to nothing.

The plastic C 111-III body in white. Originally, the wheel covers
extended well into the body and were detachable. In the final
version, their top halves were integrated into the body and
bonded onto it.

The record-breaking Diesel engine was but little modified from the
standard five-cylinder three-litre turbocharged unit. Its output,
however, was doubled, mainly by higher boost pressure and with the
aid of a charge air cooler.

Engine block, cylinder head and crankshaft were standard production parts, and most other components were close to standard.

Engine technicians Fortnagel and Obländer discussing the results of an obviously successful test.

Following double page: The exhaust turbocharger is built by Garrett in the United States. These pages show various production phases in the foundry and during heat treatment. The finished parts are scrupulously measured and X-ray tested for their metallurgic properties.

Bench testing the turbocharged engine in the course of its development. Output was 230 bhp between 4200 and 4600 rpm, while maximum torque reading showed 39 mkp at 3600 rpm.

Bottom, left: Checking an injection nozzle. Bottom, right: The exhaust turbocharger operates at 130 000 rpm and at a temperature of 1380° F (750° C).

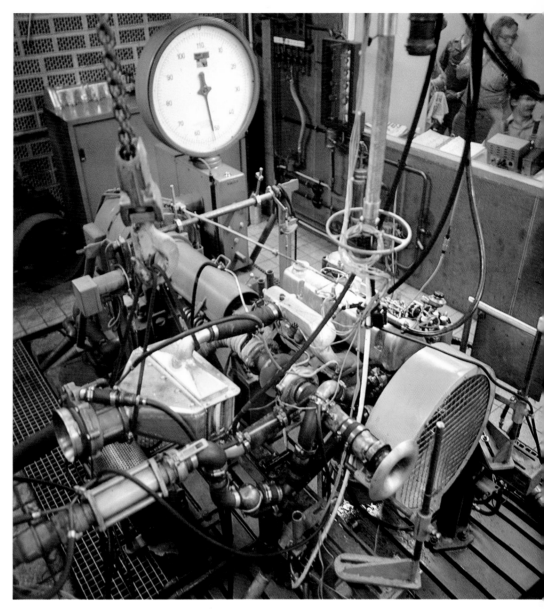

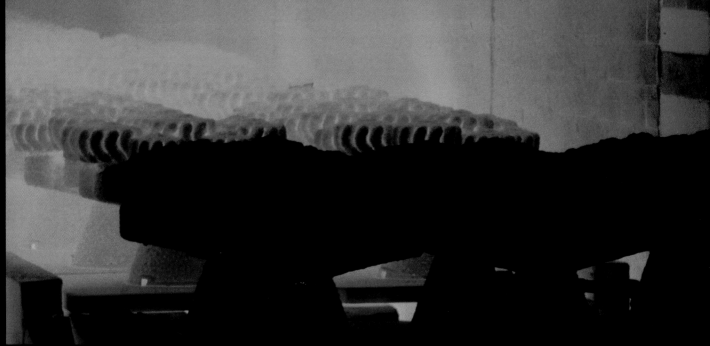

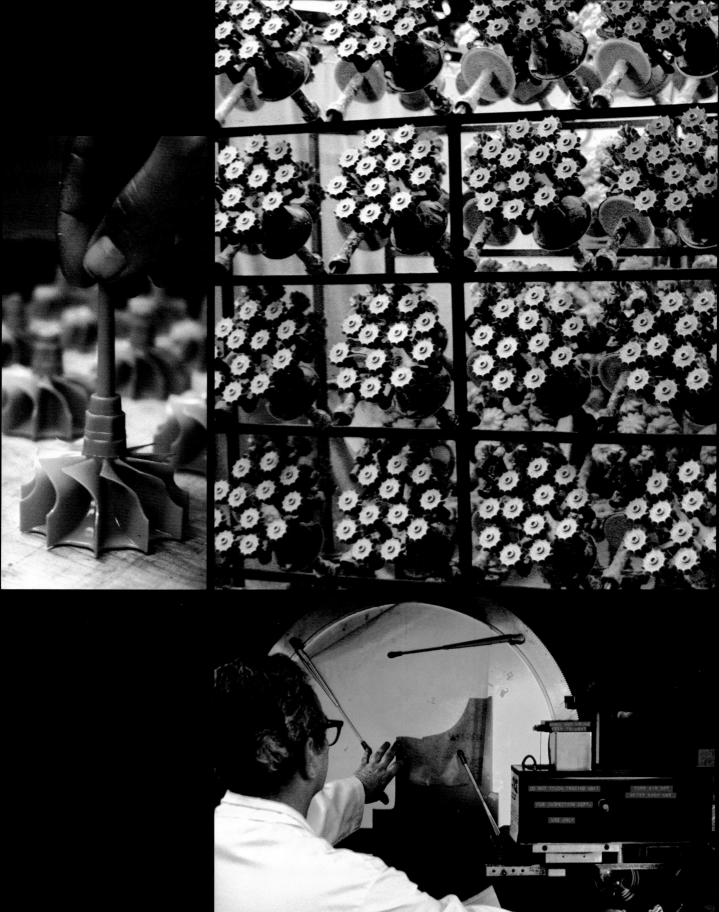

Fitting mechanical components and installing miles of wiring for the 13 dashboard instruments which transmit data by radio to the pits. Top right: Project Manager Dr. Liebold. Bottom: Tank bleeder caps at the front of the car.

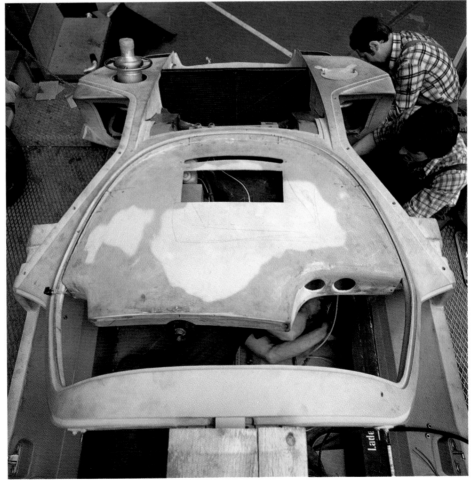

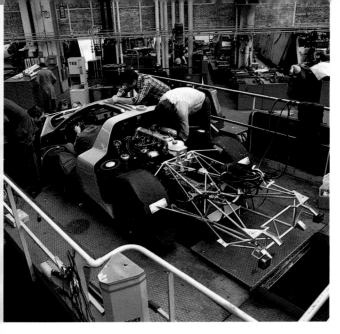

The engine is fitted last (left). A frame of aluminium tubes serves as support for the rear of the body. For comparison purposes, two tail versions with single and double rear fins were tried out (top). Fitting the windscreen (bottom).

Wind tunnel experiments continued with the completed car. For comparison purposes, a different rear fin and completely covered wheels were tested.

Left: The radio transmitter/receiver. Bottom, left: Project Manager Dr. Hans Liebold (at the wheel) discusses a test drive with development engineer Kaaden. Bottom right: The C 111-III used Dunlop racing tyres (230/600-15).

Right: First trial runs at Nardo during the winter of 1977/78.

Never before has a racing or record-breaking car offered such a high standard of comfort. Cockpit ventilation is extremely efficient, and instruments are clearly legible at speeds in excess of 185 mph. Radio contact between pilot and pit is maintained throughout the record run and actuated by contacts on the spokes of the steering wheel. The large diameter tube supplies cold air to the charge air cooler.

The gearbox can be removed without dismantling the engine. The much lightened flywheel and the clutch plate can be seen.

102

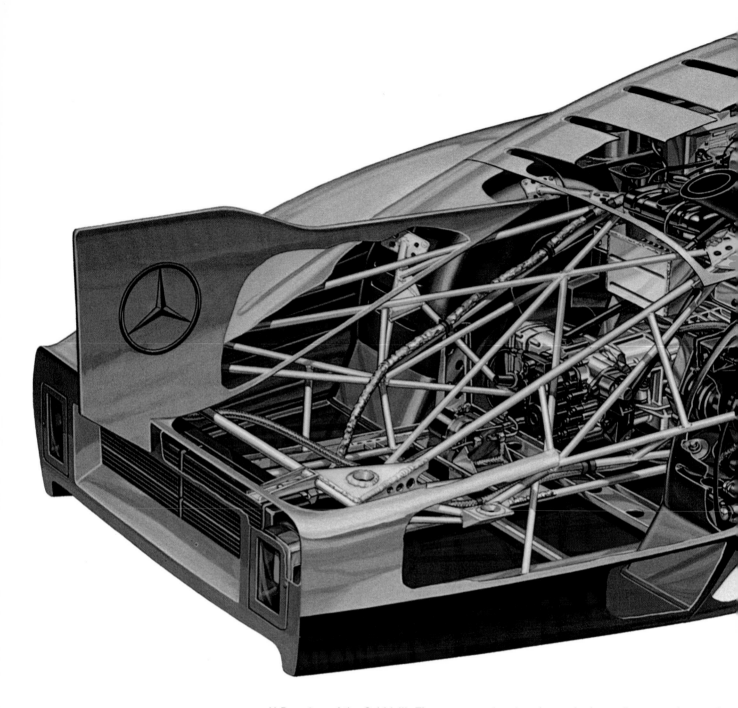

X-Ray view of the C 111-III: The cut-away drawing shows the large diameter tube passing through the cockpit. It supplies cold air to the charge air cooler. Smaller pipes branch off towards other equipment. The two fuel tanks are in front of the rear wheels. The exhaust leads into a low-pressure zone.

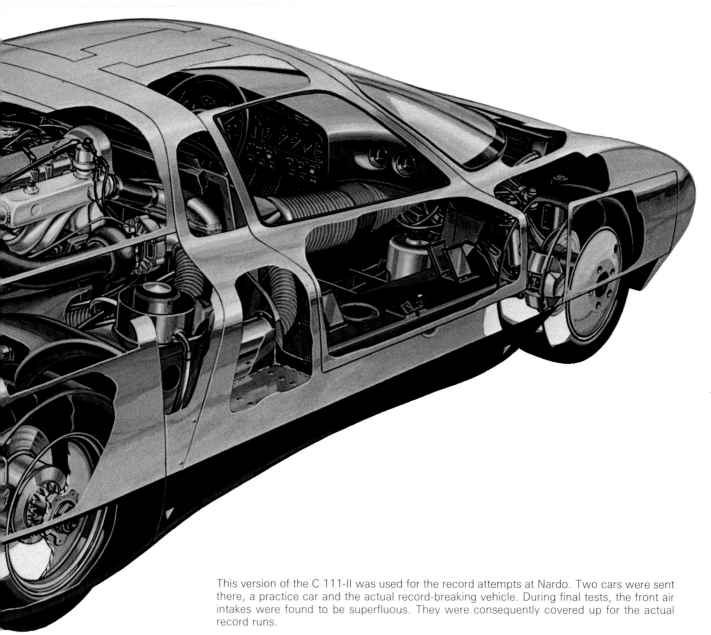

This version of the C 111-II was used for the record attempts at Nardo. Two cars were sent there, a practice car and the actual record-breaking vehicle. During final tests, the front air intakes were found to be superfluous. They were consequently covered up for the actual record runs.

THE ANATOMY
OF A RECORD-BREAKER

On April 30 1978 on the Nardo circuit, a C 111-III made an attempt on all records, from 100 kilometres (60 miles) to 1000 kilometres and from one hour to twelve hours. When it was over, Daimler-Benz held nine new world records.

Scenes from the test and record drives at the 7,8 mile Nardo circuit in April 1978: Curves at that track have a 13 degree bank. Fuel stops — including driver changes — took only about 20 seconds.

Left: Preparing the record-breaking car at Nardo. The gearbox mounting was reinforced by additional tubular attachments to the engine.

Driver change at night; Liebold at the wheel, Moch in the centre of the picture. Right: All requisite spare parts must be carried on board, otherwise records will not be official.

The pits are continuously kept informed about overall speed, lap speed, lap times, as well as all relevant data on the car's functioning, with the aid of special instruments developed by Daimler-Benz.

'The Versatile': During the reign of Professor Hans Scherenberg as Technical Director on the board of Daimler-Benz, many new models were designed, ranging from 20 ton 'Heavies' to special vehicles like the C 111. Right: Suspension specialist Göschel. Bottom: The record-breaking team. In the foreground, Professor Werner Breitschwerdt (chief of development) and the drivers Moch, Frère, Steinemann, and Liebold, as well as F. van Winsen (chief of car development). Fastest lap was 203,3 mph.

The world's most economic Diesel-engined vehicles flank the C 111-III. The latter did 17,7 mpg at an average speed of 195,7 mph. The 'Diesel miser' (left) built at Untertürkheim, returned 2739 mpg. Its rival (right), built at Sindelfingen, did 2730 mpg.

THE C 111-IV CHALLENGE

It was an attempt to break the 1979 circuit record, set by Mark Donohue on Porsche, that led to a decision by the C 111 team to modify the C 111-III and instal a 4,8 litre, V8 engine with twin turbochargers. Ten years after the first C 111 trials, the C 111-IV set a new circuit record of 250,6 mph.

A photographic gimmick by the late Julius Weitmann: The record car never looked like this!

The C 111-IV was created by substituting a 4,8-litre petro[l]
V8 engine for the Diesel unit. Expected speeds in excess [of]
250 mph necessitated additional front and rear spoilers t[o]
increase aerodynamic downforce.

Left: The 'anti-hedgehog spoiler', developed from ex[-]
perience gained during the C 111-III record runs. It is esser[n-]
tially a hinged front spoiler which gives to avoid damag[e]
when small animals are run over.

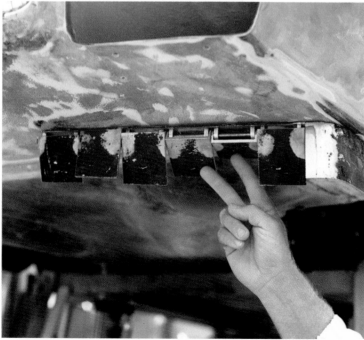

The turbocharged V8 engine was developed from the standard 450 Series engine and delivered more than 500 bhp. The front and rear of the car were further modified following wind tunnel tests.

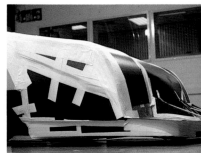

Various ways of testing the strength of aerodynamic aids. Experts on plastics (Haug, horizontal) are sometimes treated with great consideration and respect.

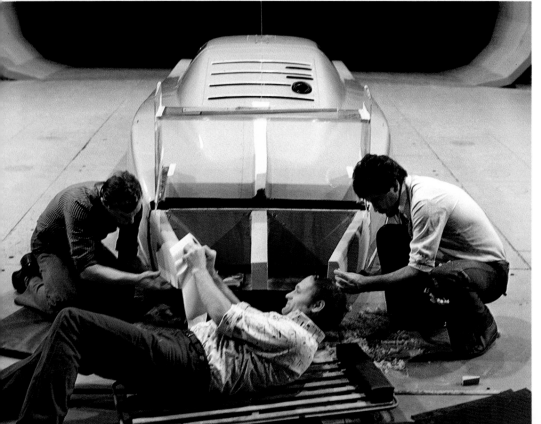

Again, various solutions were put to the wind tunnel test. Further body development resulted in improved aerodynamic downforce without increasing drag.

Surprisingly, the short, steep, front end produced a lower drag coefficient (C_R) than the long wedge-shaped nose on the C 111-III. The rear wing was later replaced by low-mounted lateral spoilers.

On April 4 1979 — precisely 10 years after the first C 111 test drives — the C 111-IV broke the unofficial world circuit record by more than 30 mph to reach an astonishing 250,6 mph on the Nardo circuit. At this speed, lateral acceleration reached 0,4 g. In order to balance wheel loads in these conditions, front and rear spoilers were made asymmetrical.

126

APPENDIX

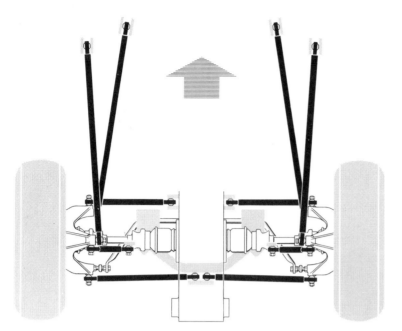

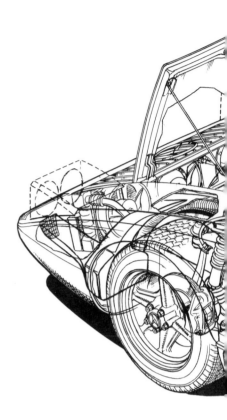

The rear suspension of the C 111 is similar in technique to that of the modern racing car. The toe-in and camber angle of the wheels can be adjusted. The longitudinal suspension arms are inclined (the frame mounting being higher than the hub mounting) in order to counteract lift during acceleration and dive during braking. Seen from above, the longitudinal arms and the transverse arms form triangles, the bases of which are at an angle to the car's axis. The transverse arms, which are unequal in length, form an angle. This puts the roll centre close to the ground with the result that the camber angle is strongly influenced by movements of the suspension.

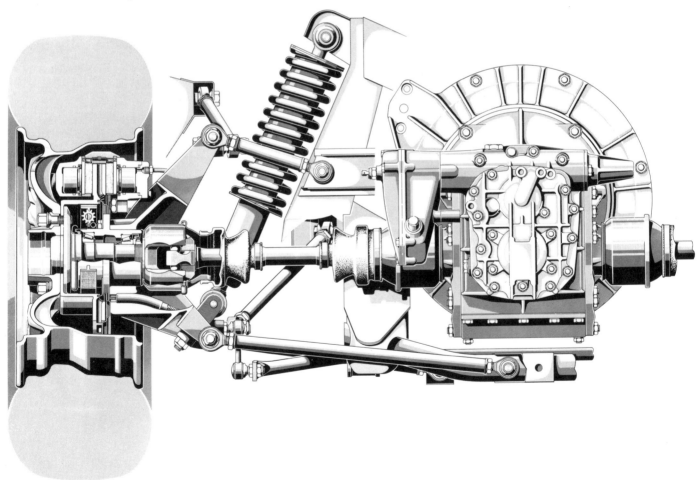

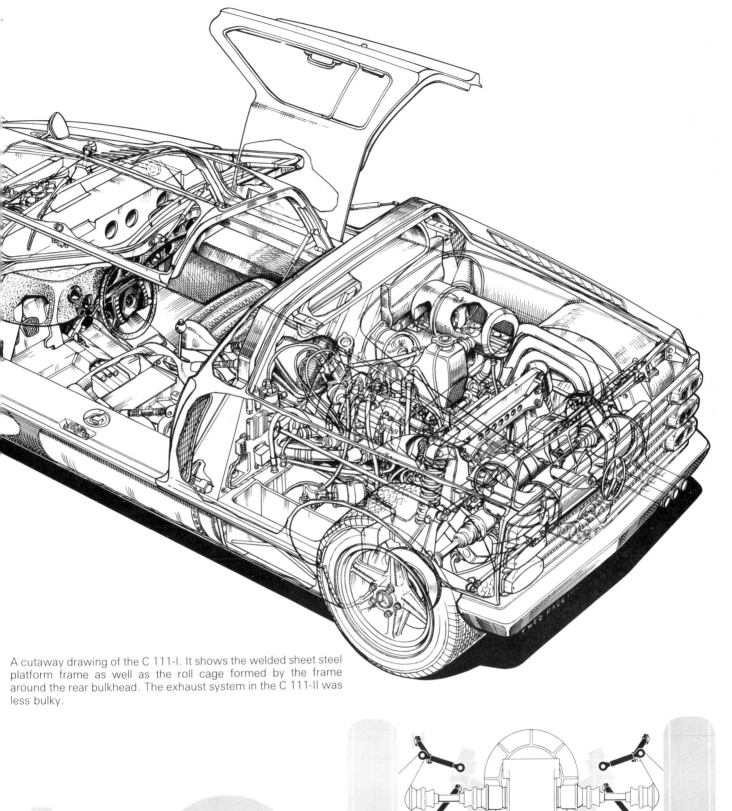

A cutaway drawing of the C 111-I. It shows the welded sheet steel platform frame as well as the roll cage formed by the frame around the rear bulkhead. The exhaust system in the C 111-II was less bulky.

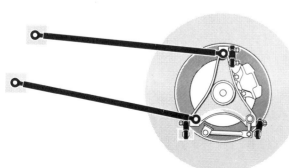

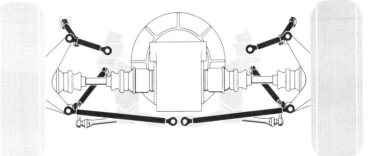

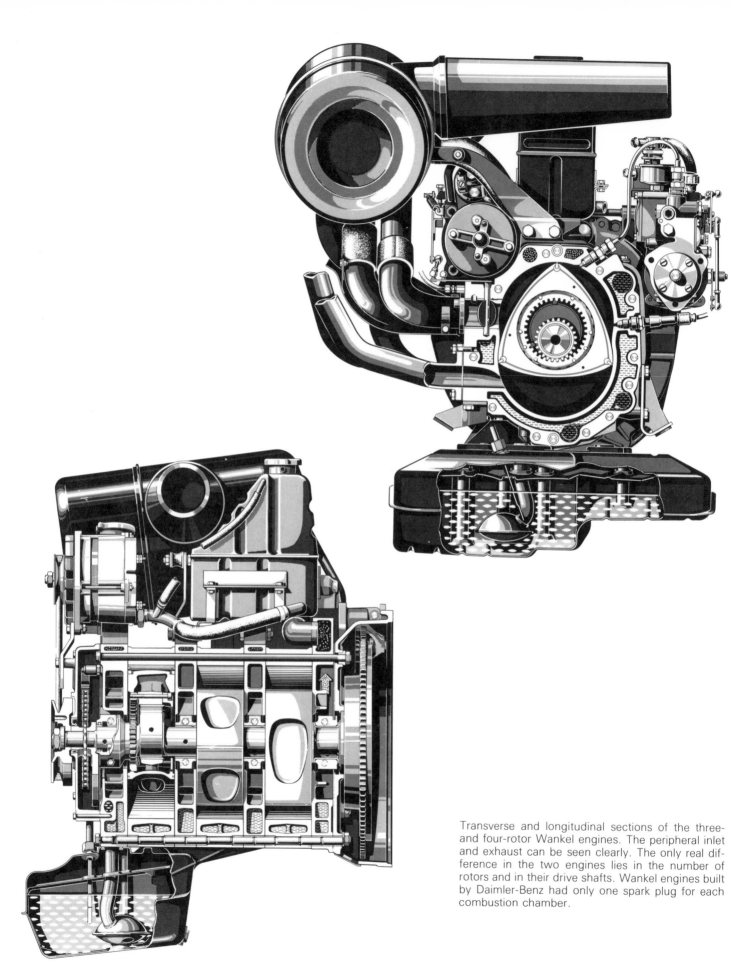

Transverse and longitudinal sections of the three- and four-rotor Wankel engines. The peripheral inlet and exhaust can be seen clearly. The only real difference in the two engines lies in the number of rotors and in their drive shafts. Wankel engines built by Daimler-Benz had only one spark plug for each combustion chamber.

		MERCEDES-BENZ MODELS C 111-I TO C 111-IV TECHNICAL DATA			
	C 111-I	**C 111-II**	**C 111-IID**	**C 111-III**	**C 111-IV**
Engine	3 rotor Wankel	4 rotor Wankel	5 cylinder Diesel	5 cylinder Diesel	V8 petrol
Chamber volume . . .	1800 cc (total)	2400 cc (total)	—	—	—
Swept volume	—	—	2999 cc	2999 cc	4800 cc
Fuel injection.	Bosch fuel injection pump	Bosch fuel injection pump	Bosch fuel injection pump	Bosch fuel injection pump	Bosch fuel injection pump
Turbocharger	—	—	Garrett	Garrett	2 KKK
Max. output	300 bhp at 7000 rpm	350 bhp at 7000 rpm	190 bhp at 4200-4700 rmp	230 bhp at 4200-4600 rmp	500 bhp at 6200 rmp
Transmission					
Clutch	Single or double plate	Double plate	Double plate	Double plate	Tripe plate
Gearbox	ZF 5 speed	ZF 5 speed	ZF 5 speed	ZF 5 speed	ZF 5 speed
Limited slip differential.	Yes	Yes	No	No	No
Overall ratio, 5th gear	3,166	2,975	2,17	1,65	1,87
Tyres	Michelin XVR 205 VR 14	Michelin XVR 215/70 VR 15	Michelin XVR 215/70 VR 15	Dunlop 230/600-15	Michelin 20/63-15 front 23/67-15 rear
		or Dunlop Racing 4.50/11.60-15 front 5.50/13.60-15 rear			
Chassis	Welded sheet-steel platform frame, plastic body shell riveted and bonded to platform frame, integrated roll-cage, two gull-wing doors.				
Front suspension . . .	Upper and lower transverse links with anti-dive device, anti-roll bar, spring struts.				
Rear suspension	Two transverse links and two longitudinal links per wheel, anti-roll bar, spring struts.				
Brakes	Ventilated disc brakes front and rear, dual circuit brake system.				
Power brakes.	Yes	Yes	No	No	No
Dimensions					
Wheelbase (in.)	103	103	103	107	107
Track (in.)	85,5/85	87/87	87/87	50/52	50/52
Racing tyres	88/85	88,5/86,5			
Length (in.)	165	175	175	212	244
Width (in.)	71	72	67,5	67,5	67,5
Height (in.)	44	44	44	41	41
Weight (cwt.)	25	25	26	28	28
Fuel tank (Imp. gal.) . .	2×13	2×13	2×15,5	2×15,5	15,5

Photolithography: Actual, Bienne
Printed by: Weber AG, Bienne
Bound by: Maurice Busenhart S.A., Lausanne

Printed in Switzerland